DANCE !!!

It's In Your

DNA

DANCE !!!

It's In Your

DNA

Dr. Jacqualyn F. Green

GRE EN TERPRIZES

Publications

Editor: Crystal Rhodes
Senior Managing Editor: Anthony Green Sr.
Cover Design: Judy Bullard
Interior Design: Green Enterprizes Publications

Library of Congress Cataloguing-In Publication Data

ISBN

978-0-9766728-5-2

GRE EN TERPRIZES

Publications

4755 Kingsway Drive Suite 308
Indianapolis. Indiana 46205
(317) 257-6773
https://www.green-enterprizes.com

Printed in the United States of America

Grandmama Mama Drama
Let the Battle Begin
© 2016 Green Enterprizes Publications
ISBN 9-780976-6728-4-5

Racial Resilience
Shattering the Silence about Race & Black Student Success in HBCU's &
PWI's
© 2009 Green Enterprizes Publications
ISBN 9-780976-672821

Spiritual Resilience:
Survival Strategies for African Americans
© 2005 Green Enterprizes Publications
ISBN 9-780976-672807

Physical, Mental & Physical Practices for Self-Determination
Available In:
Black Child Journal: Self Determination
© 2015

African American Grandparents 2014: Grandfamilies Gain Momentum
Available In:
Black Child Journal: The Black Child, Family & the Community:
National Rites of Passage Institute
© 2014

Rites of Passage: The Rite to Success for African American Girls
Available In:
Black Child Journal Special Edition: Rites of Passage Foundations &
Practices
National Rites of Passage Institute
© 2013

Overcoming the Devastation of Violence: Healing Strategies
Available in:
Healing Black Women from Violence: Reclamation And Peace
Edited by La Francis Rodgers-Rose & Zakiyyah Zai'mah
© 2011 Traces Publications

DEDICATION

Thank you to God, Oludumare, the Creator, with whom all things are possible, without whom nothing is possible. Thank you for the strength, courage, vision, and resilience to write this book. Thanks to Oshun who allows me to experience exquisite joy through this form of expression. I remain thankful for my health and for my ability to move effortlessly and with grace through this world.

Thank you to my Ancestors, who encouraged me to work hard and to do my best, but most importantly who instilled in me an ever-present sense that I could accomplish anything. Your belief and trust in me has made me experience each effort as a privilege, rather than a chore. Thanks to my dad and mom, Al & Lucile Ferguson, who taught me the value of education and often reminded me *"no one can take your education away from you."* My dad was called Twinkle Toes – because he was very light on his feet and memories of my parents dancing are etched in my mind and undoubtedly contributed to both my love of dancing and my comfort level with dancing anywhere, at any time.

This book would not have been possible without support of my family – my husband Tony, who has continued to dance with me through the years throughout the United States and in the Islands through different musical genres and a variety of styles. He often dances with me and sometimes watches me from afar as I line dance. To my sons Tony Jr. and Mikael who unanimously support whatever I do and to my grandchildren, Mikael, Kaori, & Madison whom I try not to embarrass with my desire to suddenly "bust a move"- wherever we are and whenever the mood hits.

To Earnest Barnett, one of the Washington Park dancers who provided a wonderful poetic beginning and ending for this publication. The Young at Heart Washington Park Dancers. To the dancers, particularly at Washington Park, who consistently lend encouragement to me and to each other. Many provided information for this publication, others continue to teach, reteach, support, and correct us as we attempt to learn a new dance.

To all the dancers who provided contributions for this book. To the many dancers who willingly supported this effort and provided needed and helpful perspectives regarding their involvement in dance. Without your participation, this book would have missed the incredible link between the research and the practice.

To my spiritual Godfather, Baba Karade whose words often resounded in my head as I was writing. Your guidance has continued to resonate with me as we continue on perhaps parallel journeys. The Karade family, one of writers, is truly home for me.

To Crystal Rhodes, my friend, author and inspiration for writing, as well as the editor of my materials. With your review, recommendations and continued support, you continue to shine the light on the next path that I am about to undertake. To Judy Bullard, your creativity can make this book fly off the shelves. Thank you for your effort. To those who are curious but perhaps too shy to dance, I hope that this publication will inspire you to dare to do so. After all dance, it's in your DNA!

Table of Contents

DEDICATION vi

INTRODUCTION **10**
The Flow 13

Part One **14**

THE HISTORY OF DANCE **14**

CHAPTER ONE: **15**

THE HISTORY OF DANCE **15**
    CEREMONIAL DANCES *18*
    Rites of Passage Dances *19*
    Celebration Dances *19*
    Recognition and Acknowledgement Dances *20*
    COMMUNAL DANCES *22*
    GRIOTIC DANCES *24*

CHAPTER TWO: **25**

**FROM AFRICAN DANCE TO AFRICAN AMERICAN
DANCE** **25**

Part TWO **30**

GET HEALTHIER, SMARTER & HAPPIER: DANCE . **30**

CHAPTER THREE: **31**

**AFRICAN AMERICAN HEALTH: WHY MOVING
MATTERS** **31**

CHAPTER FOUR: **35**

BENEFITS OF DANCE **35**

CHAPTER FIVE: 45

DANCING AND OLDER ADULTS..........................45

Part THREE: THE DANCERS SPEAK 48

THE DANCERS SPEAK 48

CHAPTER SIX: 51

DANCERS SPEAK 51

A FINAL WORD..97
A Tribute To The Washington Park Young at Heart
Dancers.. 100

REFERENCES 101

ADDENDUM..107
HOW TO GET INVOLVED IN DANCING........108
TWELVE TIPS FOR NEW DANCERS.....................110
AFRICAN COUNTRIES: TYPES OF DANCES
AND PURPOSE..112
DANCE SURVEY UTILIZED FOR THIS
PUBLICATION...114
MY DANCE STRENGTHS................................120
MY DANCE CHALLENGES................................121
DANCES I'D LIKE TO LEARN..........................121

ABOUT THE AUTHOR 122

ORDER INFORMATION 124

INTRODUCTION

"Everything in the universe dances. Everything has rhythm" – Maya Angelou

Have you ever heard a song or a particular rhythm that made you want to move? Did it feel as if the song was speaking to you personally? Did you make up your own movements to accompany the music? There is a craze taking place across the country at accelerated speed, particularly for African Americans! It's dancing: Line dancing, stepping, swing dancing, ballroom. Many forms of this activity have become popular.

My interest in dance is long standing and has more recently evolved into combined line dancing, stepping and ballroom dancing. Each week, I dance with a group of seniors. We number more than a hundred and on any particular day there are typically at least seventy-five (75) individuals in attendance.

Our group is composed of people ages fifty- five plus (55+). We perform in parades, compete in national contests, serve as an inspiration to residents in nursing homes, and provide entertainment at basketball games and other civic events. Many dancers identify the pleasure of the exercise as a major drawing card, and there are those who cite the enjoyment of being able to share their enthusiasm about dancing to motivate or bring joy to others.

It is curious that dancing seems to be of particular interest to middle aged or senior adults. Women seem to be attracted to this activity more frequently, than men; however, many men have joined these ranks. Dance groups have sprung up in locations like New York, Illinois, Ohio, California, Indiana, Texas, Florida, North Carolina, Georgia, New Jersey, Washington State and others. The experiences of dancers from several of these locations are presented in this publication.

Dance: It's in Your DNA is composed of three segments. In the first section of this book, the Sankofa approach is utilized. This entails looking back to history as a foundation for dance. This allows for a better understanding of the present in an effort to best shape the future. In the first segment of this publication, a snapshot view of the history of African dance and its relationship to the evolution of African American dance is explored.

In the next section, segment, the state of African American health is reviewed to substantiate why moving and exercising, through dancing, matters. Current health challenges of African Americans are detailed. This book then examines the physical, mental and spiritual benefits of dance. These advantages can aid in circumventing health issues that are quite prevalent among Black people.

The third segment of this publication presents responses from dancers regarding why they dance. Dancers share their impressions of the benefits, challenges, and experiences that are associated with the art. This part concludes with a special poem written by one of the Washington Park Senior Line Dancers.

The Addendum provides additional information regarding Tips for New Dancers, Information about African Dances, and the Survey Instrument. Readers are also encouraged to use the pages that follow to consider their dance strengths, challenges and aspirations.

Hopefully, each segment of Dance: It's in Your DNA will inform readers about the role, evolution and continued importance of dance among African Americans. Ideally, this publication will encourage readers to continue to dance or to begin dancing!

The Flow

There are mornings when you wake up
and you're moving kind of slow.
You try to move your body,
but it just don't want to go.
So you keep on moving
cause once you get the flow,
You know that you'll get
even better as you go.
The flow is a condition
that will bring you glee.
The flow is a rendition of
what it's like to be free.
The flow has rhythm
with it's very own pace.
The flow has motion
that is filled with grace.
Once you get the flow-
you stay in control.
And once you get the flow,
You stay on a roll.
Now that you have the flow
there's no need to speculate
Now that you have the flow
Just go ahead and operate!

- Earnest R. Barnett Jr. 3-12-17

Part ONE

THE HISTORY OF DANCE

CHAPTER ONE:

THE HISTORY OF DANCE

"A child brought up where there is always dancing cannot fail to dance."

- African Proverb

Dance is in our DNA. But where did dance begin? Dance and music originated in Africa, the cradle of civilization. Many remain unaware of the rich history that comes from the continent of Africa. Carter Woodson (1933) cited the denial and numerous omissions from history books, the media and educational institutions regarding contributions from African culture.

In addition to the beginnings of science, chemistry, embalming, language, and philosophy, (to name a few) Africans developed the first stringed instruments! One of those musical devices, the Goje, from Nigeria, is made of snakeskin, which covers a gourd bowl. It has only one string and is played with a wooden bow (Jade, 2013). With the invention of instruments came the joys of music and dance, both of which provided the foundation upon which significant events or needs are acknowledged.

African Dance

Africa has a rich background of culture and tradition. The continent is more than three times the size of the United States and is currently composed of fifty-two countries. African dances vary not only by country, but are often representative of numerous regions and ethnic communities. The geography and natural habitat may contribute to the type and style of dance and most tribes have a designated person whose primary role is to ensure that traditional dances are passed on to future generations. This *"dance master"* with vast knowledge of the needed rhythms, makes certain that proper movements are retained. In many instances, there is no room for improvisation. Many of these dances have been around for centuries.

African dance serves a multitude of purposes. It provides an outlet for the release of emotion. It may also serve as a means of social and artistic communication. Dance provides opportunities to demonstrate thoughts or reactions to personal or social matters, ranging from hostility to friendship. The unique movement to drums or other musical instruments allows participants to demonstrate respect or appreciation to superiors, ancestors, or others in the community (Asante, 2000). Dances also serve to demonstrate the hope for community success. Dances may be meant to inspire individuals or a community. Nature plays a valuable role in African communities. Dances may be conducted to acknowledge the passing of seasons or to request a different weather pattern. Both environment and animals are viewed with admiration and respect and are often acknowledged through dance.

African dances also emphasize different parts of the body. In Ghana, the Anlo-Ewe and Lobi emphasize the upper body, while the Nigerian Kalabari dance accents the hips. In Ghana, the Akan focus upon the feet and hands. Dances are often performed in lines or in circles, using an earth- centered approach, in which feet are positioned both wide and flat.

Gender identity, which refers to how a person perceives their gender, is reinforced by dance. Status, age and kinship may also be reflected in dance rituals. Among some Yoruba communities in Nigeria, status and age may be reflected in the order or positioning of the dancers. In Ghana, the Asante King demonstrates his position, as well as his ability, through dance.

Dance also is an important aspect in the instruction of children. Young people are taught to express emotions such as anger, grief or love through dance, songs, and drums (Thompson, 1974; Opoku & Bell, 1965).

While a plethora of rhythmic styles have evolved on the continent and are seen throughout Africa and the diaspora, a few primary types of dances are most prominent: ceremonial dances, communal dances, ritual and griotic dances. A list of many of these dances and their purpose is included in the addendum.

Types of African Dances

"Sticks in a bundle are unbreakable."

- Bondei Proverb

CEREMONIAL DANCES

"He who spends his time adorning himself knows he is going to a dance. "

-Kikuyu Proverb

Ceremonial dances are often preformed to acknowledge a variety of special occasions within a community. Dances may be held for positive occasions, significant changes, or difficult times. Designated dances may commemorate births, provide the backdrop for naming ceremonies, and inform the community of rites of passage occasions, weddings, anniversaries or funerals. These dances may also salute key people within the community.

Rites of Passage Dances

Rites of passage dances acknowledge the coming of age of a young person. The Rites of passage for Mandingo girls in Mali includes performing the *Lengin* dance. In Zambia, young girls remain in seclusion prior to the initiation to practice their steps prior to the initiation ceremony. A dance of the Maasai, the *Adamu*, performed during the male coming of age ceremonies, is also called the jumping dance. This competitive activity salutes the young man who can jump the highest in the group.

Celebration Dances

Most dances are rather complex and the dance masters are aware of the intricacies that distinguish one dance from another. While some of the traditional rhythm and movements may be consistent, the number of dancers and their formation is much more fluid and may change according to the situation. One unique dance from Ghana, a Dance of Love, is called the *Nmane* dance. This is performed during the wedding in honor of the bride. In Tanzania, I witnessed a women's Dance of Love, during which the women danced in single file throughout the community in anticipation of the wedding. Any woman who wanted to participate was encouraged to join the line at any point along the way. The activity had a striking resemblance to the Soul Train Line that exists in the United States.

Dances may also serve to welcome newcomers to a community. The *Yabara* is a West African dance of welcome. The purpose of welcoming dances is not only to introduce new members to the community, but also to demonstrate the talent and assets of the community to the newcomer.

Recognition and Acknowledgement Dances

Africans value contributions from nature. There are dances to acknowledge thankfulness for trees, forests, water or weather, which produces fertile crops. Royal dances are conducted to acknowledge individuals of special standing in the community, such as chiefs and dignitaries. Because Africans understand the power in remembering and acknowledging those who have passed on, ceremonies may be set aside to pay tribute to those who have directly or indirectly touched the lives of the living.

Special dances may be performed to honor the ancestors, people who have transitioned into the realm of the deceased. These dances may provide a forum for spiritual leaders to acknowledge the ancestors.

The purpose of dance is typically twofold: dancing may affirm a situation or condition and dance may also involve the community in the activity.

Dances that illustrate spiritual connections or religious beliefs also command a large role in African communities. Christianity is a primary religion on the continent, followed by Islam and Traditional Religions. Christianity was introduced to Sub-Saharan Africa by the Portuguese and Dutch in the 15th century. Those on the coastal regions of the continent were often severely punished for practicing their indigenous religions. Inland Africans more removed from the invaders of their land, continued their spiritual practices until the 1900's when many countries were infiltrated by missionaries and colonizers.

By this time, many Africans had already converted to Islam, which became prevalent in North Africa since 500 AD, having been introduced to the continent through Greece. Traditional religions, often regional, included diverse people such as the Serer of Senegal, the Yoruba and the Igbo of Nigeria and the Akan of Ghana and the Ivory Coast. Numerous practices, which grew out of African religions, are practiced throughout the diaspora. Music and dance accompany these demonstrations of faith.

COMMUNAL DANCES

*"When you play the flute in Zanzibar
all Africa dances. "*

-Zanzibar Proverb

African dance typically occurs in a communal gathering and serves to demonstrate the vitality within the group. Communal dances may be held to observe the nature's change of seasons, the successful completion of community ventures, or the key roles within the community.

Dances may also equip members for community roles. War dances provide physical and psychological preparation for war. Some dances, such as Nigerian *Korokoro* dances are a form of martial arts (New World Encyclopedia, 2016).

Drums continue to play a vital role in the life of the community. The drum is a means of communicating emotions and connecting with those within the range of the sound. The sound of the drums serves to unite the group and drums contribute to a sense of solidarity among all members of the community.

RITUAL DANCES

"We have not inherited this land from our ancestors; rather we have borrowed it from our children."
                    - African Proverb

Ritual dances are perhaps the oldest of African dances. Ritual dances reinforce the significance and beliefs of society. Sacred ritual dances are often religious and serve as an expression regarding African ancestral reverence. Ancestors, who are considered to live on in the spirit world, play a very significant role in African culture. Connections with the ancestors are maintained through song, dance, and prayer. The elders typically lead ritual dances.

Ritual dances may be held to celebrate life or to commemorate death. Each of life's transitions may be observed through music and dance. The *Mbira* dance of Zimbabwe is representative of this type of dance. It is danced to call upon the ancestors, to remove droughts or floods, to honor anniversaries of the deceased or to seek guidance in disagreements in the family or the community. In Nigeria, the Owo Yoruba lead the *Igogo* dance. This dance is performed during burial ceremonies (New World Encyclopedia, 2016).

In addition to paying tribute to God or the ancestors, ritual dances also have a therapeutic function. Healing is sought by Hausa women through dance. The Alun tribe deals with disorders in women by dancing in ceremonies. Among the Kalabari, dance and song are viewed as important components of healing (Lewis, 2017).

GRIOTIC DANCES

"If everyone is going to dance, who, then, would watch?"
-Cameroonian Proverb

A griot is a historian, a storyteller. The depth and significance of the griot as a storyteller can be summed up in this African proverb: *"When a griot dies, a library has been burned to the ground."*

Griots hold a key position and play a significant role in the African community. They, as keepers of the culture, internalize key facts about their village. The African tradition consists largely passing down information orally from generation to generation. Storytellers may be tasked with reciting the history of a family or community. This practice is often accompanied by music and/or dance. The Lamba dance was reserved for Malinke storytellers in Senegal to preform a particular history.

"Nobody is born wise." – African Proverb

CHAPTER TWO:

FROM AFRICAN DANCE TO AFRICAN AMERICAN DANCE

"When the Music Changes, so Does the Dance."

– African Proverb

French, Dutch, British and Spanish colonizers transported Africans through the Middle Passage to the United States and the islands in the Caribbean. Once sold and dispersed to plantations, enslaved Africans were severely punished or killed for practicing their language, religion, or dance. Attempts were made to erase any connection with the Motherland.

Dancing was initially prohibited. However in secret, some dances remained and others emerged among the enslaved Africans, such as the Calenda. This dance was conducted using two lines facing one another. Men stood on one side and faced women in the other line. With an approach avoidance movement and rhythm, the dance quickly sped up and progressed to thigh slapping, kissing and other contact. This fast rhythm alarmed the plantation owners and the dance was banned from the behaviors allowed for enslaved Africans. The Calenda, however, inspired other dances such as the Cakewalk, which mocked plantation owners. The Charleston was also an outgrowth of the Calenda. Later, certain forms of dancing by the enslaved Africans were accepted for the entertainment of the plantation owners and their guests. (Crawford, N.D).

Once slavery was abolished, dancing became more widespread and commercial. As early as 1897, two African Americans, Bert Williams and George Walker, played in a vaudeville house in New York, which featured the Cakewalk and seven couples in "fancy dress." Bill Bojangles Robinson, a legendary tap dancer, was given his start by the four Whitman sisters, in 1905. This all Black group included dancing, songs and skits.

The Whitman sisters toured for three decades in vaudeville circuits. At the Lafayette Theater, in Harlem, the *Darktown Follies* production included tap, ballroom and acrobatic dances such as the Strut, Tango, Mooche and Ballin' the Jack. In fact, theatrical impresario Florence Ziegfeld viewed these shows and attempted to replicate those impressive movements at his theater. In the 1920's and 1930's, all black Broadway shows emerged. Dances such as the Slides, Marches, Struts, Shimmies, Strolls and Slow Drags became popular.

In 1933, a forum *"What Shall the Negro Dance About"* was held in Harlem by the Workers Dance League. In 1937, dance gained additional notoriety when James Weldon Johnson, author of the Black National Anthem, gave a speech at the opening of the American Negro Ballet at the Lafayette Theater in Harlem (Manning, 2014). Various forms of dance gained more popularity in a variety of venues.

Katherine Dunham, legendary choreographer and dancer, utilized African dance to develop movements used in modern dance today. She and her company entertained audiences on Broadway, in Hollywood, on cross-country tours and later performed internationally.

Alvin Ailey choreographer and founder of the Alvin Ailey American Dance Theater in 1958, also incorporated traditional African dance in his multifaceted dance performances, which included ballet, jazz modern and spiritual music. Both of these musical icons have had a profound impact upon dance in the United States and throughout the world.

Dancing became more of a public phenomenon with the emergence of dance shows on television. Dick Clark featured dance in the 1960's on TV's American Bandstand. On August 6, 1960, Chubby Checkers introduced the Twist to Bandstand viewers. The dance became a national craze.

During the 70's many viewers gravitated to Soul Train to watch African American teens dance. Later, street dancing and break dancing emerged and became prevalent across the country. Many forms of these dances, including popping, locking, and krumping, are very similar to African dance movements. The motions, which accent a particular region of the body, and the delivery in the midst of a circular audience, are similar to dance practices on the continent (Crawford, N.D.).

The African influence on the evolution of dance in America continues even today. Step shows, preformed by African American fraternities and sororities are often held to entertain the public. The quick motions and simultaneous movements tend to mesmerize audiences. These carefully choreographed steps incorporate gestures associated with African dance. A dance with a major influence upon stepping is the African Gumboot dance (Hillbring, 2017). Unfortunately, many African Americans, old and young, are unaware of this connection and do not realize how African culture permeates current day practices.

"The hottest music and dance always comes from home."
- African Proverb

DANCE! It's In Your DNA

Part TWO

GET HEALTHIER, SMARTER & HAPPIER: DANCE

CHAPTER THREE:

AFRICAN AMERICAN HEALTH: WHY MOVING MATTERS

"Those who do not find time for exercise will have to find time for illness."

- Edward Smith Stanley

Health and movement, such as dance, are closely aligned. People who have an active lifestyle tend to experience fewer illnesses. This author suggests that those who embrace *"the ribs and the remote"* tend to have a greater incidence of high blood pressure, strokes and heart disease (Green, 2005). This lack of mobility, which applies to many African Americans, makes Blacks more vulnerable to a variety of diseases. Some report that particular illnesses have been alleviated or lessened with a change in lifestyle. Weight control, for example, also a benefit of physical activity, helps to prevent numerous ailments (Center for Disease Control, 2017).

What are major health concerns for African Americans? The Office of Minority Health, an arm of the Center for Disease Control (CDC, 2016), reports that high death rates in African Americans result from heart disease. Nearly fifty-percent (50%) of African

31

American men and women have some form of cardiovascular (heart) disease. Several conditions contribute to heart disease, including diabetes, hypertension (high blood pressure), and obesity. In addition to contracting diseases at higher rates, African Americans are more likely to die from those illnesses (CDC, 2017).

Approximately thirteen-percent (13%) of African Americans, nearly five million Blacks, twenty years of age or older, have been diagnosed with diabetes. This rate is more than twice that of European Americans (American Diabetes Association, 2014). Obesity is extremely prevalent among African Americans. Approximately 69% of men and 82% of women are overweight or obese (CDC, 2017). More than 40% of African Americans have hypertension. African Americans have the highest rate of hypertension of any group in the world!!! Research indicates that African-Americans may carry a gene, which makes them more vulnerable to salt, or a salt sensitivity, which increases the risk of high blood pressure (American Heart Association, 2017). As little as one half teaspoon of salt can elevate the blood pressure! Think about that the next time you add salt to a meal, particularly one that you have not yet tasted!

While some health conditions are associated with social or economic conditions, others may be attributed to life style choices.

Among African Americans 50-64 years of age, twenty-four percent (24%) are identified as at risk due to smoking cigarettes and thirty-five percent (35%) are viewed as at risk due to immobility (CDC, 2015; Behavioral Risk Factor Surveillance, 2015). The number of couch potatoes is increasing with greater numbers of "creature comforts' that contribute to a more passive lifestyle. Today, many shoppers make purchases on line rather than going to a store. The exercise from walking throughout a store or in a parking lot may be a helpful positive health maintenance activity.

Young people have become more sedentary, particularly when playing electronic games or utilizing cell phones. Back in the day, when I wanted to talk with my best friend, I walked over to her house! This practice is quite foreign today! African American youth are contracting more diseases and illnesses at younger ages than their white counterparts. These diseases that are acquired earlier progress more rapidly, leaving the adult with a more severe form of an illness.

Movement could benefit those of all ages. According to the Center for Disease Control (CDC, 2015), African Americans are living longer, particularly those sixty-five (65) and older. For this age group, the death rate has decreased about twenty-five percent (25%). With a longer life span, it is even more critical that individuals implement strategies to ensure a greater quality of life.

Movement can serve as a preventative measure. The Center for Disease Control (CDC, 2015) recommends one hundred and fifty (150) minutes of physical activity each week. According to those standards, only eighteen percent (18%) of African Americans are viewed as physically active! Moderate intensity aerobic activity such as brisk walking or dance can positively affect the health of those who participate. Exercise can also improve mood and reduce anxiety (CDC, 2016). African Americans need to MOVE! Dancing can be a perfect activity to promote good health.

"Disease and disasters come and go like rain, but health is like the sun that illuminates the entire village."

– African Proverb

CHAPTER FOUR:

BENEFITS OF DANCE

"Health is the main thing."

– Swahili proverb

Dancing provides advantages in all areas of life. Any movement provides physical, mental and spiritual benefits for the individual involved. Dance has been utilized as a therapeutic tool to address conditions such as depression or eating disorders. Dancers also tend to be more involved in other positive activities such as healthy eating and other forms of exercise.

Dancers reap numerous benefits from this activity and research verifies that dancers tend to benefit MORE through dance than from other forms of exercise such as biking, swimming, walking or tennis!   If you have ever considered an activity that would be fun filled, improve your health, and widen your social circle, you're reading the right book! Dancing is a preferred means of elevating health!

Dance offers some unique advantages. Dancing is a way of remaining active and being physically fit. It energizes and revitalizes the dancer. The dialogue between the music and the dance creates an energy that promotes good health within the dancer. The following quote from Baba Olatunji, master African Drummer and dance instructor, describes the impact of dance:

> *"The health benefits derived from African dance go far beyond the gratification you get from dancing for relaxation or celebration. African dance is grounding–it brings you down to earth and that is the first realization of knowing where you stand. You learn how to relate your whole self, body and soul, to Mother Earth, that which supports you. You dance to the beat of a drum, obeying the natural law of being in rhythm. And in doing so, you arrive at a place where you are in total control of yourself."*

Attempts to be grounded and healthy physically, mentally, and spiritually can be achieved through dancing. It is a fun way of tending to your temple.

> *"If you close your eyes to facts, you will learn through accidents."*
>
> – African Proverb

Physical Benefits: Getting Healthier

" Take care of your body it's the only place you have to live."
– African Proverb

If you have talked with any line, step or ballroom dancers, you might be aware of the enthusiasm with which they talk about the activity. They are quite likely to invite you to dance sessions, or to talk about the joy that they experience when dancing. Research has found that dancers experience numerous benefits from that activity.

In general, most dancers report feeling good and noting added energy as a result of dancing. Exercise has been known to raise serotonin and endorphin "feel good" levels. Dancing certainly reinforces those positive feelings. It's not surprising that dancers express favorable sentiments. In addition to the elevated mood, another advantage of higher serotonin and endorphin levels is an increase in one's immune system.

Dancing offers some preventative properties, which can serve to ward off particular diseases and ailments. It can increase good cholesterol levels, which allow control of blood sugar. According to the

American Council on Exercise, the chance of developing cardiovascular disease or high blood pressure is reduced in dancers (Matthews, 2009). Dance also reduces body fat, which contributes to lower incidents of ailments such as cancer, diabetes and heart disease (Knowles, 2017).

The invigorating activity of dance also strengthens lung capacity. Movements that are required in dancing improve the heart and cardiovascular system. Dancing produces a more rapid heartbeat, which results in increased blood flow and oxygen to the muscles. Because it is a muscle, the heart becomes stronger, with additional use. The advantage of this activity is evidenced even after completion of the exercise. When resting, dancers have a slower heart beat than non-exercising individuals. This lowered capacity is because the heart has become more efficient and does not have to work as hard (Adler, 2014).

Dancing may contribute to better sleep habits Dancers have been found to experience a more relaxed sleep. Dancing can also alleviate insomnia. The physical benefits of dancing contribute to a more productive and healthy lifestyle. While producing hormones that help one to feel better, dancing also reduces the potential for certain ailments.

Mental Benefits of Dance:
Getting Smarter

"Dancing stimulates the mind, body, & soul. It has been proven to increase cognitive strengths and prolong life. That is the miracle of dance. "

- Lai Rupe'

Wanna get smarter? Who knew that this could happen through dance! The research about the mental benefits is noteworthy. One of the most remarkable findings about dance is associated with thinking and memory. Dancing has been found to enhance brain functioning at all ages and *particularly* with older dancers (Alpert, 2010). You can literally dance yourself "SMARTER!" With regular dancing, the brain tends to work faster and connections within the brain become stronger.

Dr. John Ratey, associate clinical professor of psychiatry at Harvard Medical School suggests that dancing can increase memory and thinking abilities. He also views dance as a mechanism that can improve academic functioning. Students might consider dance as a way of maintaining an alert mind! Dr. Ratey suggests that dancing is exercise for the brain, which contributes to greater mental performance (Ratey, 2008).

The phrase *"use it or lose it"* is applicable here. Researchers have found that mental abilities increase with additional use of the brain. Exercising cognitive "thinking" skills increases the ability in the brain to process information. The split second decisions often required in dancing serve not only to create new connections in the brain but also assist in sharpening the existing brain cells. Learning *new* patterns in dance and other activities is a recommended strategy for stimulating brain connections. Several studies have been conducted to identify the relationship between physical exercise and brain activity. When comparing tennis, golf, swimming, bicycling and dancing *only* dancing improved mental acuity (Powers, 2010)!

Dancing is especially helpful to brain activity because kinesthetic, rational, musical *and* emotional brain functions are utilized simultaneously (Powers, 2010). This activity contributes to dancers having a more active, productive, mind! Dancing may also contribute to an increased ability to concentrate. Focusing upon dance steps, music and positioning of self, partner and other dancers requires being aware of what's going on around you, as well as changes in the music.

Dance has additional therapeutic properties. Dance therapy is used to alleviate anxiety and depression. It has also been used to treat panic disorders. There are numerous mental benefits of dancing. Dancing has been practiced as a healing activity. This sounds quite similar to the rationale for some types of African Dance that were described in Part One of *Dance, It's in Your DNA*.

Involvement in dance also increases avenues for creativity. Dancing lends to opportunities for greater self-expression and personal development. Those who dance tend to receive compliments for their involvement from other dancers, friends, and family. Dancers who perform may receive positive comments from audience members. These positive strokes are undoubtedly encouraging and may influence the dancers' desire to continue with this positive outlet.

Who would not want to improve their brain functioning? Greater awareness of this advantage might encourage more people to get on the dance floor!

"Wanna Get Smarter? DANCE!"

Spiritual Benefits of Dance: Getting Happier

"Tell me the last time you danced and I'll tell you the last time you were happy."

- African Shaman Quote

Studies have shown that dancing to music, even for as little as five minutes, can increase happiness (Halliwell, 2016). This is undoubtedly due to the increased serotonin and endorphin levels described in the physical benefits section. Dancers often describe feeling good, and report enjoying the activity *before*, *during* and *after* dancing. According to dance psychologist, Dr. Peter Lovatt of University of Hertfordshire, dancing stimulates emotional centers in the brain, often resulting in what he terms " *uncomplicated happiness.*" He suggests that this aerobic activity provides an atmosphere for the release of pent up emotions. Dancing provides a space to clear the mind and refresh.

Fitness expert, Matt Roots (2016) attributes this happiness to other chemical changes in the body. He suggests the changes in body chemistry may be related to dance causing a reduction in levels of the stress hormone – cortisol. This hormone contributes to greater relaxed feelings and an aura of peacefulness or happiness. Dance also provides a release. Dancing is cathartic. Pent-up emotions can be released during this aerobic activity (Roots, 2016; Lovatt,). Dancing may even provide more opportunity for spiritual connections.

Many describe feeling "free" when dancing. This freedom undoubtedly refers to freedom from worry, freedom from mundane considerations, and perhaps even, freedom from pain. Dancers have reported that regular exercise has decreased the discomfort from pre-existing physical ailments! Such freedom may allow individuals to connect more comprehensively on a spiritual plain.

The spiritual nature of dance is widespread and has been well known to Native Americans, Australian Aboriginals, and to Africans. These groups have danced to pay tribute to God, to request rain, to salute nature or the seasons, and/or to acknowledge ancestors. Some dances function to describe historical events or tell stories regarding the life of an ancestor. Dance provides a mechanism for keeping the history alive and for passing on the information to future generations.

Spiritual dancing practices vary widely and range from Praise Dancing to meditative states when dancing to honor God or a Higher Power. Some cultures use dance to attain trance states. Dancing is described by certified dance movement therapist Brauninger (2016) as a means for attaining a peaceful state of mind. The peace described in "movement therapy" is viewed as a spiritual release, as well. For many, this calm, peaceful, state is a ripe environment for enhanced spirituality.

Different states of consciousness have been found to be attainable through dance. Some describe dancing as a spiritual experience in which they feel light, while others describe an out of body experience. Frequently, individuals describe dance as evidence of total surrender. The ability to access spiritual thoughts, feelings or connections may be more prevalent in this state (Kieft, 2014).

The calmness and contribution to a space which stimulates openness may lead to greater understanding of self, others and God. What a remarkable benefit of dancing.

"Do you not know that your body is a temple of the Holy Spirit who also lives in you?"
                                        - Corinthians   6:19

44

CHAPTER FIVE:

DANCING AND OLDER ADULTS

"A woman is never old when it comes to the dance she knows."
                              -African Proverb

While dancing is advantageous for participants of all ages, some particular benefits exist for older people. Research has shown that for seniors, dancing makes a significant difference in some of the normal aging challenges. One of the advantages for the adult dancer is a slowed aging process of the body. Activity helps the cells to renew and remain more vibrant.

The regularity of the movements strengthens bones. Bone Density which is often a concern regarding older adults is less prevalent among the older dancer. Due to increased bone strength the potential for osteoporosis is also decreased. Dancing may also be beneficial to maintaining balance, which is often a difficulty faced by older people. The movement burns calories, which can may allow one to have that extra piece of cake without guilt or unhealthy weight gain.

Dancing contributes to improved posture and quicker reaction times in older adults. The improved reaction times undoubtedly reduce the number of falls and accidents, which can be major hazards encountered by this group. Older dancers experience greater flexibility and lower body muscle endurance. Dancers are stronger and have more aerobic power than non-dancers of comparable ages (Kattenstroth, Kalisch, Holt, Tegenthoff, and Dinse, 2013).

Often, among aging adults, a noticeable difference in handwriting occurs. This change is often due to a lack of steadiness in the hands. Because dancing provides increased muscle control over both the hands and feet, it can reduce these occurrences! Many older adults and some young ones too complain about arthritis. Dancing lends to improved circulation and lubrication of the joints, which serves to prevent arthritis. Dancing is now being used to treat people with Parkinson's disease.

A study of older adults found that while most physical activities did not offer any protection against dementia, the singular exception was DANCING! Older adults who danced frequently *lowered* the risk of dementia and memory loss by seventy-six percent (76%) (Kattenstroth, Kalisch, Holt, Tegenthoff, & Dinse, 2013; Allen, 2017). For those who have already contracted Alzheimer's or Dementia, dance is used to improve short term and long-term memory, as well as to improve overall quality of life among seniors (Powers, 2010).

The social community formed by dancing has been found to be valuable to older adults. Line dancing may be of particular significance to the older dancer, as a partner is not required. Many widows, widowers and/or single dancers are free to participate in this activity. A study of older women who were line dancers found that they were more likely to be involved in the community, charitable work, and in national sports events than those who participated in other exercise activities (Nadasen, 2008). The social community formed by dancing has been found to be beneficial to older adults. Older people with social activities and connections tend to experience less depression.

"You don't stop dancing because you grow old, you grow old because you stop dancing."

- Adapted from George Bernard Shaw

Part THREE

THE DANCERS SPEAK

DANCE SURVEY PARTICIPANTS

Again, special appreciation goes out to all those who participated in this study. Your answers were both informative and precise. By reading your experiences, hopefully, others will be inspired to put on their dancing shoes. Thanks to each and every one of you for sharing your time, your insights, and your encouragement to others to get on the dance floor!

~Jackie Armistead
~Jeanette Barnett
~Christine Barnett
~Earnest R Barnett Sr.
~Evelyn Berry
~Gary Boards
~Sherrie Boards
~Patsy Brown
~Willie Brown Jr.
~Rhoda Capers
~Mauris Emeka
~Loree Fant
~Lynda Ford
~Janice Gardner
~Tony Gee
~Jay Gee
~Goldie
~Mikael Green
~Edward Griffith
~Sandy Griffin

~Kevin Heeter
~Isha Hutchinson
~Lorraine Jackson
~Ellen Lane
~Michelle McCartha
~Raymond Martin
~Nancy Nelson
~Evelyn Pace
~Mildred Paris
~Marie Pollard
~Ron Ragland Sr.
~Sherri Ragland
~Evelyn Robinson
~Hershell Scott
~Lynda Scott
~Nadirah Shareef
~Gracie Simmons
~Micky Swagger
~Vanessa Summers
~Shirley Ward

It is music and dancing that makes me at peace with the world... And at peace with myself..."

–Nelson Mandela

CHAPTER SIX:

DANCERS SPEAK

"We dance for laughter, we dance for tears, we dance for madness, we dance for fears, we dance for hopes, we dance for screams, we are the dancers, and we create the dreams."
— Albert Einstein

Survey Design

Forty (40) African Americans were asked to complete surveys regarding their dancing experiences. Individuals were selected from known line dance classes, internet dance groups, selected ballroom, step and line dance instructors and individuals who were recommended by other dancers for survey completion. Responses were collected in two ways. Some completed a written survey and others chose an electronic format available on line through a website. Participants represented several cities in Indiana, Ohio, New Jersey, Washington State, California & Texas. The following information is based upon the responses that were made by survey participants.

Participants were asked to report their gender, which allowed a determination regarding the level of male and female participation.

Gender

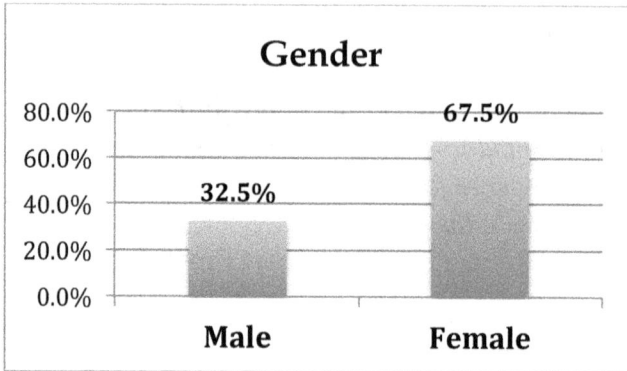

Two thirds (2/3 's) of the participants were women and one third were men. This number seems reflective of a variety of dance groups and social events in which Black women typically outnumber men by nearly two to one.

Participants provided information regarding their age. Age ranges were provided which included under twenty-five (25) to eighty plus (80+). No participants fell in the lowest age range categories or the highest age range, which included those who were eighty and over.

Age

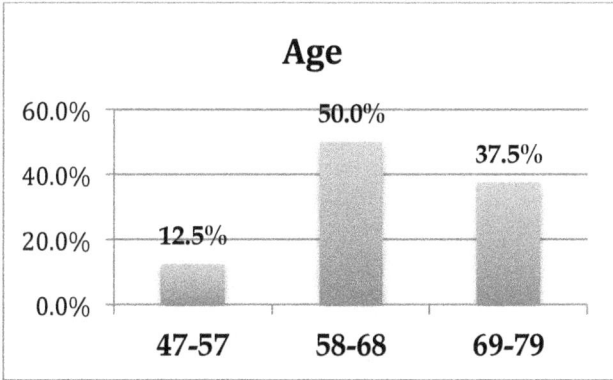

Participants ranged in age from 47-79. Most dancers fifty percent (50%) were represented in the 58-68 age group. Older dancers were targeted for this survey as advantages of dance in older adults was a major focus.

Employment

Participants were asked about former or present employment or retirement status. The employment status was varied among participants. While most were retired, or semi-retired, several continued to work. Dancers reported a wide range of careers, from self-employed and management to education and sales. This suggests that dancing attracts participants from a host of different disciplines. The occupations (past and present) that were represented among the dancers are depicted in the following chart.

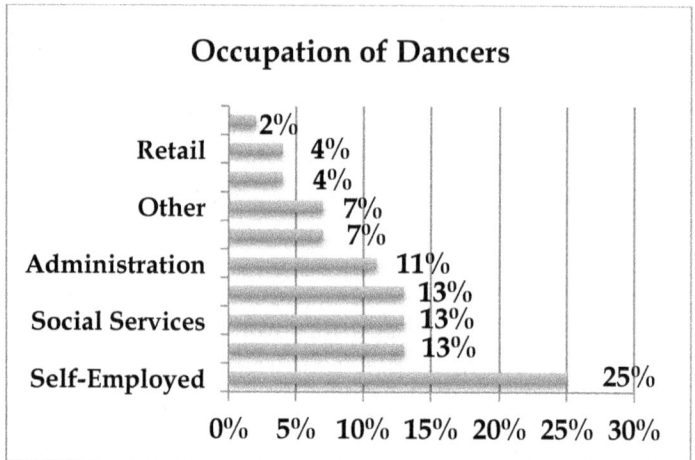

Occupation of Dancers

Category	Percentage
	2%
Retail	4%
	4%
Other	7%
	7%
Administration	11%
	13%
Social Services	13%
	13%
Self-Employed	25%

0% 5% 10% 15% 20% 25% 30%

Most (25%) of the dancers were entrepreneurs or self-employed. Equal participation was distributed between those in management (13%), social services (13%) and government (13%). Dancers who reported administrative positions composed 11% of the participants.   Nearly 7% of the dancers worked in health services. Five percent (4%) worked in computers or retail (4%). Only one educator (2%) was included in the study. The involvement of three individuals (7%) was placed in the "other" category.   This included Amtrak Train, General Motors, and a Basketball volunteer.

The occupations (past and present) that were represented among the dancers are depicted in the following chart.

OCCUPATIONS OF DANCERS (Past & Present)			
Self-Employed Fashion Design Owner Insurance Tax Advisor Childcare Business Owner (pre school & real estate) Small Business Author Soul-Line Dance Instructor Public Speaking Business Owner	**Management** Manager Business Management Supervision Natural Products Research & Project Management Industrial Supervision Black Economic Research Center Assistant Director	**Social Services** Corrections Officer Youth Services Director Bilingual Community Specialist Counseling Mental Health Therapist	**Government** Government Federal Civilian Employee Post Office State Representative Retired Army Officer
	Administration Administration Administrative UPS Administrator Executive Secretary Telecommunications	**Health Service** Respiratory Therapist Registered Nurse Psychiatric Nursing	**Computer** IT Project Manager Information Technology'
Other Amtrak Train Attendant Retired General Motors Basketball Volunteer	**Retail** Bicycle Stores Sales	**Education** Education	

"When you dance, your purpose is not to get to a certain place on the floor. It's to enjoy each step along the way." – Wayne Dyer

Perhaps these dancers are continuing to enjoy each step – along the way.

Length of Time as a Dancer

Participants were asked how long they had been dancing. An unexpected outcome was found regarding this question. The majority of the dancers either reported a brief length of time in dancing (5 years or less) or identified that they had been dancing for a very long period of time (31 years or more). Six (6) to ten (10) years of dance was reported by over 26% of the dancers and slightly more than 5% of the dancers reported having danced 11-15 or 26-30 years. No dancers identified dancing in the categories of 16-20 years or 21-25 years.

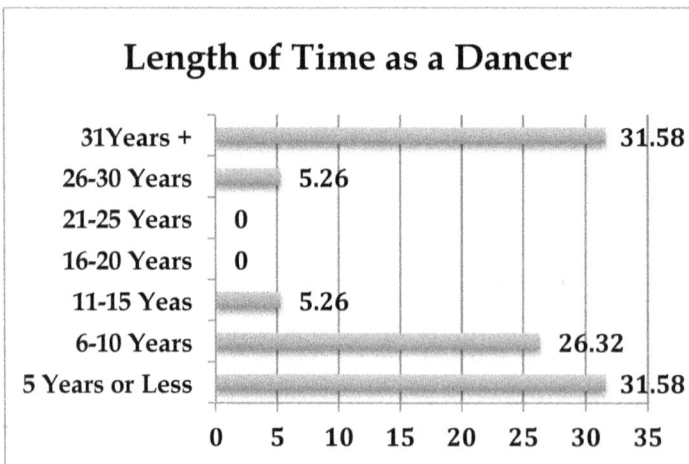

Length of Time as a Dancer

Category	Value
31 Years +	31.58
26-30 Years	5.26
21-25 Years	0
16-20 Years	0
11-15 Yeas	5.26
6-10 Years	26.32
5 Years or Less	31.58

Type of Dancing

Dancers were asked about the type of dancing in which they participated. Many of the respondents were involved in line dance classes across the country. Answers provided by the respondents seemed to reflect that most dancers participated in line dancing as well as another type of dance. It is possible that once participants began line dancing, exposure to and interest in other types of dance occurred.

Nearly all dancers (97%) participated in line dancing. Ball Room dancing was the next highest category with nearly a third of the dancers (33%) involved in that activity. Approximately twenty five percent (25%) of the dancers called themselves "Steppers." Swing dancers composed about slightly more than twenty percent (20%) of the respondents.

Twelve percent (12%) of respondents suggested other specific dances. These responses included African dancing, hip-hop, square dancing, fox trot, and slow dance. Additional responses included old school step, aerobic and solo dancing. One respondent reported that any dance that they could do was a favorite type of dancing.

Type of Dancing

97.44	25.64	33.33	20.51	12.82
Line Dancing	Stepping	Ball Room	Swing Dancing	Other

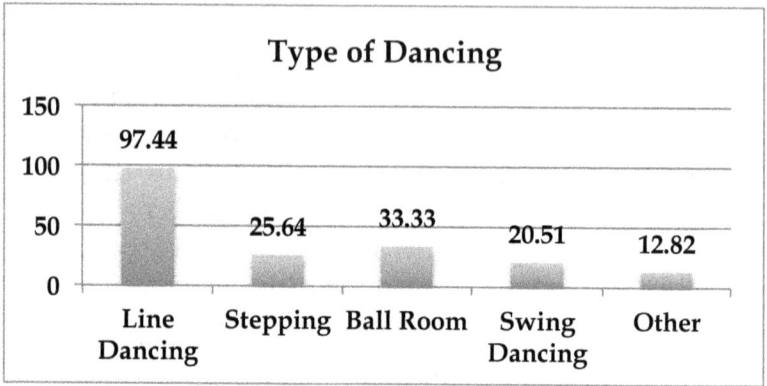

Frequency of Dancing

It's very clear from the reports of the dancers that those who dance tend to dance a *lot*! Nearly half of the respondents dance three to four times a week. Typical dance sessions may last for an hour or two hours. Approximately a quarter of the dancers indicated that they danced twice per week. Some of the dancers (13%) reported daily dancing! Others, nearly eleven percent (11%) dance weekly. Fewer dancers, nearly six percent (6%) dance either twice a month or once per month.

Frequency of Dancing

Category	Value
Once a Month	2.7
Twice a Month	2.7
Once a Week	10.81
Twice Per Week	24.32
3-4 Times per Week	48.65
Daily	13.51

0 10 20 30 40 50 60

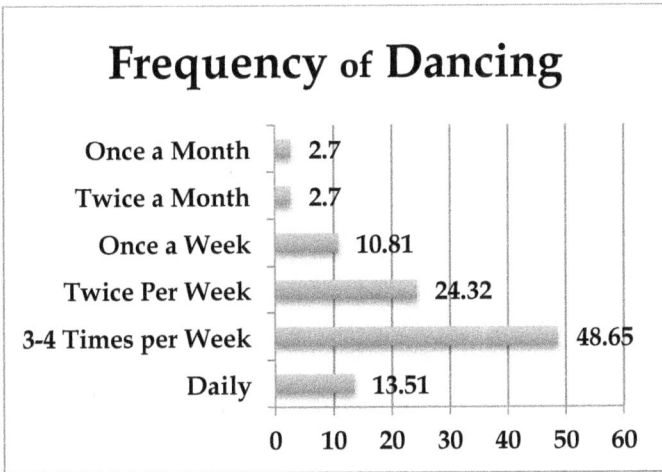

Favorite Dance

Participants were asked to identify their favorite dance and to identify why they liked that dance. Favorite dances were quite varied, which perhaps illustrated the diversity within the group. Most dancers (16) indicated that line dancing, in general, was their favorite and that it would be difficult to select a specific dance. Among those who made selections, the line dance performed to the Twenty-Four Carrot music was the most popular with four (4) responses. The line dance that accompanied the Backyard Party song followed with three (3) individual selections. Ballroom, Chicago Stepping, Slow Dancing and the Cha-Cha each received two responses. The remaining participants selected a vast array of dances.

The dances identified were:

1. Baltimore Good Foot
2. Cupid Shuffle
3. DB Groove
4. Happy
5. Heritage
6. Hitting the Folks
7. I Blame You
8. Old Fashioned Hustle
9. Signature
10. Swing Dancing
11. Temptations Cha-Cha
12. Terminal Reaction
13. You're My Star

What I Liked About the Dance Selected?

Dancers then responded to why a particular dance was their favorite. Responses ranged from the joy felt from a particular dance to the health and social benefits of participation. The top three responses included: (1) the dance, (2) the music, and (3) the partner aspect. While some really enjoyed that line dances require no partner, others liked the involvement with a partner in the dances that they selected. Statements regarding the dance selections are as follows:

The Dance

- I like the smoothness of the dance.
- The Lube Dance is one that I really enjoy.
- It was one of the first dances that I learned that I really, really, liked!
- The Cha-Cha is a four step dance, which is incorporated into many different line dances. That steps in that dance make it easy to learn other dances.
- There is a line dance for any type of music.
- Line dances give you the opportunity for more freestyle.
- It's simple and rhythmic. Anyone can do it.
- The symmetry involved in the movements really makes the dance beautiful to watch.
- I love the easy dance steps.
- I love the steps that make you want to move.
- It is a high-energy dance with many turns and fast movements.
- Line dancing allows you to dance to all kinds of music- country & western, gospel, hip-hop, and jazz.
- Line dancing offers you the opportunity to learn a wide variety of dances.

The Music

- I like or love the music or the music is great (6 responses here)!
- The dance is easy on the knees and leg muscles.
- The music is very upbeat and makes me want to really move!
- It's cheerful and upbeat, especially when we stop in the middle and start high fiving each other.
- The music is as uplifting as the dance!

Partner

- You don't need to have a partner to dance! (6 responses here)!
- You get to hold someone close.
- In dance class, you meet great people and you learn new dances. You don't need a partner and you can dance as much as you like.
- Chicago Stepping is a wonderful couple/partner style of dance for my husband and I.
- I don't need a partner and I love that there is always a new dance to learn.

The Movement

- I enjoy teaching others how to move like me!
- Dancing gets people moving.

- The music makes me want to move.
- I like the moves that accompany the song.
- There are quick & precise movements through out music.

Challenge

- Some dances are more complex and present a degree of difficulty. I enjoy attempting to tackle those dances.
- The dance has four distinct parts that are difficult, yet fun to learn. When I learn them I feel as though I've mastered a hard task.
- Line dance steps constantly change and this challenges the mind.
- I love that it's a difficult dance and it takes a lot to try to learn this dance.

Physical

- The dances that I select are easy on the knees and leg muscles.
- Dancing keeps you fit and the music remove the stress of life.
- I dance for exercise & good health.

Creativity

- With some dances you can add turns and inject moves that fit the music. I like that freestyle opportunity.
- You can be creative with dance steps

Fond Memories

- My late husband loved music and dance. I continue the enjoyment.
- It's the dance I first learned in my growing up years

Social Benefits

- Also, I love that there is really no age limit in line dancing (or most of the dance world). My dance friends range in age from 20's to 80's.
- Friendships made.

How I Got Interested in Dancing

Dancers shared how they became involved in dancing. Many were influenced by family, friends, and in social situations in which others motivated them to begin dancing or dance more often. Responses are presented as follows:

Family

- My parents danced and taught me to do it at an early age.
- My son-in-law told me to call a friend and the friends' stepmother was involved in line dancing. I called her

and she told me where to go that Monday. I went to Washington Park on 30th Street and that's how I got started.

- I've always loved dancing. I come from a family that LOVES to dance. I learned to "Swing" from my beloved Mother. She is Puerto Rican, so I also learned to Salsa, Cha-Cha, Merengue, etc. from her, along with my aunts and uncles. As a youngster/teenager, I always tried to keep up with the latest dances. My love for dancing increased as I became older.
- The Washington Park group danced at my sister's job at a nursing home and she really enjoyed it. She told me about it and wanted us to learn to line dance!
- My late mother and grandmother loved dancing. My mother did clogging with groups and I watched the fun the groups had. When I retired I wanted to find a group to enjoy this activity with.
- My parents danced and talked to me about dance at a very young age.
- My brothers and I have always danced. I can't remember when we didn't dance.
- My wife started country-western line dance for exercise. We started in California in the early 90's.
- My parents danced in the living room when I was two. I practically learned to dance before I could walk!

Peers / Others

- When I saw other people doing that dance, I wanted to learn.
- I have always been interested in dancing, with rhythms, so when I observed seniors doing what I like to do and having fun doing it, I was sold.
- I was at a party where they were doing a dance I'd didn't know. I googled line dances and saw "Chuck Baby" and wanted to learn it. I found classes near me and the rest is history.
- I saw the dance that I really like and wanted to learn more dances than I knew at the time.
- I saw a ballroom demo. That got me started.
- With Line Dancing, I saw members of *Young At Heart* at a dance and was really impressed with the number of dances they were doing that I had never seen. I started in the class the very next week.
- I began dancing at the YMCA.
- I started dancing at a Senior Citizens Club.
- I have always loved dancing but only danced the 2-step occasionally. When I went to my last class reunion, my classmates did one line dance: The Electric Slide; I had forgotten how to do

it and vowed to and did start taking
Line Dance lessons within that month.

Friends

- Unable to play baseball, basketball or bowling due to knee pain so a friend suggested line dancing.
- A friend recommended that I try line dancing.
- I got interested in line dancing about 12 years ago. I was invited by a church member to come to visit. Visited, loved it and haven't stopped.
- A friend from church needed men in their class and I volunteered and have loved it since then.
- Friends who were interested in dancing encouraged me to do so.
- I attended lots of social functions where dancing occurred. I wanted to participate.
- I have been dancing in some form or another from an early age. Dancing with friends at house parties and sock hops. I was also in a dance group with the high school marching band.

Fun & Enjoyment

- I have always enjoyed the fun of dancing.
- I love the way it looks. It's easy (somewhat).

- I started dancing just for the fun of it while in the tenth grade.
- I have always enjoyed dancing even as a kid.
- I have always loved dancing.
- I lived in Georgia 3 years and was associated with line dancing there and fell in love with it. We visited nursing homes during Easter & Christmas.
- I watched American Bandstand when I was 12 years old. I am 70 now. I have always liked to dance. It makes me feel good.

Personal Goals

- When my twins went to college, I realized that I needed a new me.
- I have always been a dancer since my teen years, and I love how the styles of dance today can conform to your level of activity. There is always a way to improvise your steps and movements. And there are many dances to choose from to fit your abilities.
- I broke my leg and needed an exercise that allowed me to move at my own pace frontwards, backwards, and sideways to strengthen my leg.
- I would line dance to de-stress from work. After getting the Wobble etc., I started wanting to put my own flair to the dance, and after a while I noticed I was being shunned and excluded by

some other dancers although I wasn't really trying to be included. I realized that the best way to do this and have fun is to start my own.

School

- In grade school. I liked the music and practiced dancing for hours on end. Then in college, this was a regular weekend activity.
- We had a mandatory class in 4th grade where we learned all types of dancing. I kept on dancing after that!
- I have been dancing since childhood....I went to dances at St. Rita's, which is where dances were held for youth to attend!

Unsure

- I don't know for sure, I have been dancing since I was a child.

What Physical benefits have you noticed from dancing?

Participants were asked about any physical changes had noticed since they began dancing. Overwhelmingly, the benefits of increased stamina and energy topped the list. Dancers felt stronger and developed increased self-confidence that affected not only how they felt about dancing, but in other areas of their life! An added plus from performing an activity that was enjoyable was weight loss. As older people tend to have a slower metabolism, often weight gain can be problematic. Nearly a third of the dancers (27%) experienced weight loss.

Many dancers reported that they enjoyed the exercise. Some identified being able to sleep very comfortably. A general sense of "feeling good" not only mentally, but also physically, was a common thread among dancers as they described benefits to their heart, lungs, coordination and balance. Responses are included here.

PHYSICAL BENEFITS

"If you stumble, make it part of the dance."

- Unknown

Strength & Endurance

- I have increased stamina (7 responses here)!
- My energy level is higher (5 responses here)!
- I have more endurance (4 responses here)!
- Dancing strengthens my legs.

- My endurance level is high, we can still dance the night away and we STILL enjoy many activities and vacations with family and friends.
- Dancing has strengthened my body.
- I get increased stamina not only from dancing but also in calling out the dance steps.
- I have experienced Improved stamina and greater strength.
- I have built stamina and can dance for long, long periods of time.

Weight Lost

- I lost weight (5 responses here)!
- The most important physical benefit is the fact that I have lost weight.
- I've lost weight (15 pounds and maintained it for the last 3 years).
- Dancing helps with weight control
- I have lost weight and am not out of breath when I dance - like I first did when I started
- My knees don't hurt. I have lost weight.
- It also helps burn calories to keep my weight down.
- It helps to prevent obesity.

Exercise

- I like the exercise (4 responses here!

- I like the fact that dancing gives me the exercise that I need.
- A form of exercise, moving the body to help stay in shape.
- Dancing is a very good form of exercising and I rather do that than working out.
- It keeps me on the move all the time! It's good exercise.
- Exercising and rapid breathing increase levels of healthy living.

Sleep

- I sleep better at night (4 responses here)!
- I sleep well.
- After dancing I am more relaxed and sleep better.

Joints

- My joints stay loose (3 responses here)!
- My joints seem to remain loose. I typically feel good
- Your joints are less stiff. You are able to move more freely

Heart & Lungs

- My heart and lungs are stronger.
- My heart is functioning has improved.

- Dancing gets your heart rate up. It's energizing and I sleep better.
- Because I like the higher energy dances, I have been forced to keep in good cardio shape to execute the dances the way I want to.

Other

- I'm 70+ years and in pretty great shape and I attribute it to dancing.
- Dancing is a way that I stay in shape.
- Through dance, my blood oxygen level has improved.
- I like to sweat- this cleanses my pores.

Mental

- It boosts my morale.
- It also lets me use my mind in thinking beyond daily use.
- Helps in keeping the mind alert.

Balance

- I think I have better balance than most people my age.
- My body senses balance when I dance - which is exercise of my core.
- Dancing has helped me to improve my balance.

Muscles

- I had to stop dancing for a while and noticed that the muscles in my legs felt better when I returned to it.
- Dancing works muscles that are not used often enough.

Good Health

- I typically feel good.
- Dancing is great exercise that helps to eliminate hypertension, heart attacks and arthritis. It also helps with Alzheimer's because you have to learn and remember the new dance steps.
- For my age I think it is a reason that I'm in such good health!

Brain

- I get a chance to give my brain a workout by learning new dances and remembering the old.
- Dancing has helped me to think and process information easier.

Enjoyment

- I just enjoy dancing.

Circulation

- It fosters good blood circulation throughout my body.

Coordination

- I have better coordination due to dancing.

Social

- I enjoy meeting different people!

Calories

- When dancing, I burn excess calories.

MENTAL BENEFITS

"The only dancer you should compare yourself to is the one you used to be."
- Unknown

Participants were asked what mental benefits they noted from dancing. An overwhelming majority of the dancers reported mental improvements such as memory improvement, concentration, and being mentally sharp. Dancers also reported dancing as a positive stress reliever. The social benefits of dance were also noted. Several described their dance group as a "family." Their mood, which reflected "happiness," was also identified.

Thinking

- The main mental benefit is that I think more clearly and I multi-task a lot more. My memory is better because my thoughts are clearer.
- I continue to keep my brain active by learning and remembering the dances.
- I remember moves and specific movements required to dance.
- I am more alert because of dancing.
- I am able to remember the dances once the music starts. Dance recognition sharpens my memory.
- Mostly just thinking of the moves. It keeps your mind sharp.
- Mentally dancing keeps my mind young and fit and I believe it will help me from getting dementia and Alzheimer
- Our style of dancing requires you to learn steps and beats to different tempos of music, this constant learning, definitely helps with memory retention
- It makes me think and concentrate all the time. Learning steps to each part of dance- then remembering to put the right steps to right parts of the dance requires a lot of thinking and concentration!!!

- I'm not sure but remembering all the steps to line dancing has to maintain and improve your mental capacity, especially with seniors. Continuing to learn new forms of dance keeps me mentally sharp.
- Dancing helps me to redirect my thoughts. It helps me to think more clearly
- Dancing keeps my mind sharp.
- By remembering steps, it keeps the mind sharp.
- Line dancing has improved my mental acuity
- Learning and remembering dance steps helps to keep my mind sharp

Memory

- Dancing has improved my memory (5 responses here)!
- My memory is improved by remembering line dance steps, the name of the dances, and the name of songs.
- My memory has been helped by identifying which beat in the music is used to begin dancing.
- I have Increased mind memory.
- This constant learning, definitely helps with memory retention.
- Learning and remembering the dances has helped my memory.

- I have an increased capacity to remember the sequence of dance moves and steps.
- That is impossible to say, but I am remembering a lot of line dances.
- Memory is required! If you don't use it you lose it!

Stress Reducer

- I think it helps reduce the stress from everyday life.
- I get stress relief from dancing as much as I do.
- Dancing helps to remove stress from all areas of your life.
- Dancing is my primary de-stressor.

Social

- It's also a good way to converse with people who share common hobbies.
- and it gives me the opportunity to laugh a lot as I fellowship with friends.
- I met a positive group of people whom we consider family. We do cruises together and go out to dance like family. We are not "friends"; we are family and don't have or do "drama."
- The camaraderie gives me a sense of well-being. It has also increased my circle of friends.

Calmness

- Dancing keeps me calm.
- Dancing releases endorphins that have a calming affect that helps with pain.
- Dancing helps with depression because you are constantly moving.
- Dancing serves as a mood elevator.

Self Confidence

- Dancing has given me the self-confidence to learn and teach dances.
- Dancing contributes to confidence in all areas of my life.
- I feel that if I can learn how to dance, I can learn anything.

Relaxing

- Dancing is relaxing.
- Mentally, dancing relaxes me.
- Dancing also helps to relieve stress.

Positive Attitude

- Dancing helps me have a positive outlook.
- You can't be depressed and dance too.
- This gives me the chance to be FREE without any titles etc. I don't allow others to tell me anything negative

about my dancing because to me, that defeats the entire purpose of doing this.

Happy

- Dancing keeps me happy.
- I had been involved in politics for a very long time and had decided to pull back from it after serving 19 years as an elected member of the Passaic School Board. I was a little concerned about how I would fill my time once I decided to retire in 2013. Now I am so VERY HAPPY I retired when I did. I'm more upbeat and always excited about meeting new people and learning new dances. I'm upbeat and positive about my life.
- Looking forwarded to the time when we will dance again brings emotional joy and anticipation.

Focus

- I think dancing increases my ability to focus.
- Line dancing has improved my concentration.
- It keeps my mental faculties active because I have to concentrate to remember the steps of each dance.

Muscle Memory

- Dancing keeps muscle memory intact.
- I have developed muscle memory.

Escape
- I can really get into the music and the movements and leave any problems behind.
- You can forget problems for at least an hour.

Mindful
- Dancing keeps me in the moment.

SPIRITUAL

"Dancing is the hidden language of the soul of the body."
– Martha Graham

Dancers indicated that dancing provided an opportunity for them to feel gratitude. . Dancers described the ability to have good health and to dance as a gift. Many described a feeling of peace when dancing. This vessel for peace made it possible to experience a deeper spiritual connection with God. The opportunity to share the "gifts" with others through entertainment media opportunities or nursing home visits was also reported as a spiritual experience.

Gratitude

- I am reminded when I dance of how grateful I am to God for the ability to move and to have good health.
- God designed our bodies for movement and he shows us "we can do all things thru Christ." Exercise, dance, move and do some things we don't think we can do.
- My faith in GOD is not because of dance, the freedom of dance is a gift from GOD.
- I thank the Lord for allowing me to move and dance.
- Dancing reminds us that good health is such a wonderful precious gift from God. I have learned to treasure that gift and always give thanks for this favor from God.
- I thank God for giving me the mental ability and the physical ability to be able to learn to dance and continue dancing for a long time.
- Knowing that God gives the power and strength to dance!
- Not only dance for self -improvement but also "dance unto the Lord" Rejoicing & Praising Him for who he is.

Peace

- I feel more at peace when I dance.
- Dancing is a great stress reliever.
- Line dancing has increased my spiritual awareness for peace, unity and fellowship.
- Dancing gives me peace and joy.
- I am calm and able to connect the higher spirit, which is the God to me.
- I don't have any tension when I am dancing. I am calm and able to connect with the people around me.

Sharing

- You feel good when you learn a dance by following a person. Great when the dance is committed to memory and wonderful when you can teach a dance.
- Rewards of sharing with others (my Saturday class goes to needy family program).
- It also provides a lot of Fellowship opportunities.
- Dancing with others provides a spirit of fellowship!
- It's such an inspiration when we visit nursing homes to see the patients become lively and try to dance with us. I consider this my ministry because I believe God gave me the inspiration to dance. Our group takes our craft to nursing homes.

None

- There were 5 "none" responses.

Positive People

- The people that we dance with are very positive.
- Positive benefit to yourself & others
- I don't know if you'd call it Spiritual, but dancing is my "happy place". If I'm down or get the blahs, dancing ALWAYS brings me up!
- Dancing keeps me grounded! I leave my troubles while dancing and experience fellowship among the line dancers!

Stress Relief

- Dancing frees my mind.
- Dancing reduces my stress.
- Dancing relaxes me. It settles my mind.

Other

- It's about family. When you loose all your siblings, I've lost four (4) from diabetes, your mind, body and soul changes.
- Dancing keeps me grounded! I leave my troubles while dancing and experience fellowship among the line dancers!

- Not only dance for self -improvement but also "dance unto the Lord" Rejoicing & Praising Him for who he is.

Joy

- It brings joy to your life to share with others, which makes them happy as well. Dancing also provides a sense of a positive family connection. I'm often told that this is a ministry that beings so much joy to the life of those whom we touch.
- The camaraderie, laughing, lifting of spirits is undeniable.

Mindfulness

- Dancing also makes it easy for me to BE in the present moment, and not occupy my mind with the past or the future.
- Spiritually, dancing is good for the Body, Mind and Soul and it keeps me connected to my true Essence and helps me to be Spiritually grounded.

Relationship with God

- Spiritually, I feel closer to God. My relationship is very good and open. I can talk to him at any time of the day and feel good knowing that I can do that.

Heritage

- In African dances I feel connected to my heritage.

Taking Care of the Temple

- I believe that God wants us to take care of our bodies He BLESSED us with. For me, line dancing is assisting me in doing my best to make healthier choices and take care of myself.

Breathing

- When dancing, it's easy for me to remember to breathe deeply and do it often.

"A person is a person because of other people." - Zulu Proverb

DOWNSIDE

Participants were asked to identify any downsides of dancing. The overwhelming response to this item that there was no downside! Most dancers did not experience any shortcomings as a result of dancing. Several respondents used this opportunity to caution those interested in dance to take things slowly and to avoid over-exertion. The most important "equipment" needed by the dancer was identified as the shoes. Several stressed the importance of having adequate footwear. The expense incurred by the "traveling dancers" was also addressed, particularly in view of the desire of many dancers to travel to a variety of dance activities. Some reported the difficulty in having to make a choice regarding which dance events would fit into their budget.

None

- No was the most frequent response. At least sixteen (16) respondents indicated that there was no downside to dancing. A few comments in which participants elaborated a bit more, are included here.
- I have no downsides to dancing. I just try to be consistent in whatever I do.
- No, unless it takes you longer to learn the steps.
- None- you just have a lot of choices to pick from.

Limitations

- Sometimes I'm not able to dance when or as frequently as I would like.
- Some movements require quick and repetitive steps- but with practice (repetition) it comes.
- Know your physical limitations. I dance with different age groups and know

some of the dances the 30's-40's age group do are not for me at 62.

- One must do everything in moderation, know your body.
- When you start, you will be tired. Move at your own pace.

Over-Exertion

- Sometimes I can over exert myself and be sore.
- The older you get is the soreness from too much dancing (smiles).
- Sometimes, I experience sore muscles.
- It is possible to dance so often and for so long that you create some soreness in the feet, ankles, and legs.

Possible Injuries

- Some dances can be challenging on different parts of the body!
- You may have knee problems – pain.
- You may have pain in your lower back.
- Don't do repetitive steps too often.
- Your feet, legs, and knees may hurt.

Footwear

- Proper footwear and foot care probably should be emphasized more in dance classes.
- Proper shoes will help.

- You have to wear good shoes. Dancing can cause foot problems.

Social

- People get upset with you when you don't want to dance with them.
- We do not have enough male partners to dance with. I'd like to see more men involved in our group.

Finances

- The expense of traveling, classes, and wardrobe should be considered.
- It can be financially daunting when you see so many events all over the country and I want to go to practically ALL of them. I've had to set up a "line dance budget.

Difficulty Keeping Up

- So many dances come out almost every day that it is difficult to keep up.
- If you don't dance you, it makes it difficult for you to keep up with what's going on. The more you move, the better you feel.

Other

- Everyone has their own style and the positive is just to move! Keep moving and the music moves you.
- Others may find the more challenging dances intimidating, but there is a place for ALL abilities in the Dance community.

Limited Space

- I think that there is too much politics, crab in the bucket and critiquing going on out there. There is room for everyone, even if you don't particularly like their style, you can always find another space on the floor.

Loss of Sleep

- The only downside is that sometimes I stay out a bit late dancing and my sleep for that night is cut short. But luckily this only happens occasionally.

"You can start late, look different, be uncertain, and still succeed."
                                        - Misty Copeland

DANCER STORIES

"Great dancers are not great because of their technique, they're great because of their passion."
        – Martha Graham

_____

On the final question of the survey, dancers were asked if they would like to share a particular experience that they had encountered while dancing. Participants shared funny stories, insights, tips, surprises and nostalgic sentiments as a result of this activity.

Passing it on...
        I think my favorite experience was watching a group of almost 100 people perform a routine that I came up with by myself.

Crashing the Party
        Once I was out of town in a hotel. I was with a conference but there was a wedding party in the same hotel. I heard their music playing down the hall and ran down the hall, joined them on the dance floor and left immediately when the song was over. I had crashed my first wedding!

Spreading Joy

When we go to Nursing Homes, the residents get a kick out of the group and they come and dance with us. This is very rewarding.

Dropping it like it's lukewarm?

There is a dance where I can get very low to the floor. I was told by one of my fellow line dancers that one day when I do it - I am going to get stuck!

Just remember to ENJOY

It's just dancing, so don't be so serious. Have fun, laugh at your self when you mess up, (and you will) jump back in when can and just dance.

Stars in My Eyes

My first overnight line dance event occurred about 10 months after joining Step4Step Soul Line Dancing. We traveled in 2 vans from New Jersey to Cleveland, Ohio. When I saw how many people from all over the country were there, I was stunned. One of my favorite pictures is the one a friend of mine (it was her first out of state event, as well) took while we overlooked the ballroom on the first night. To see almost 1,000 people doing the same dance at the same time was AWESOME!

I was hooked! The fellowship and camaraderie I saw displayed there has grown by leaps and bounds since that trip. I saw people helping others "on the wood", "mini-workshops" in the lobby, the hallway, etc. It helped cement my commitment to this lifestyle. I now have friends all over this country and I am so BLESSED!

Where am I?

Once I was dancing and in the middle of the dance- I had a mental block while doing my favorite line dance.

A Dose of Reality

When I first started, I didn't believe that there were so many steps to learn. I complained about it going out the door. I was complaining so loudly, a guy heard me, tapped me on my shoulders and said..."You can't learn everything in one practice, keep coming back." I kept coming back and it got easier and easier. I started out as a beginner, but now I'm a line dance instructor and I love it! As a matter of fact the guy is one of my students!

Under the Eye of the Camera

My husband and I were at a dance that was being recorded, and the dancers rotated around the floor, every single time we passed the camera, we missed a step. A step that we both can do in our sleep, we laughed and kept it moving.

The Solo Dance

Sometime we miss steps in a dance by going into your own private zone grooving because the music is so great and then get back in step with the dance. I call it "Doing Your Own Private Solo."

You Can't Touch This

When I dance, I compensate for my knee replacements. When I do a turn, I lose new dancers when they try to duplicate my steps. I slide my feet and when you do your own thing, people follow and say you messed me up even though they are just learning.

No words...

One of my dance students tells me that dancing has helped her improve a lot, but she cannot tell me how. Hymmm.

The Legacy

My 20 month old great grandson mimics our dance style- cha-cha, ballroom, etc...looks a lot like his grandpa rubbed off.

You don't know me

When people see me initially and do not know me, they assume I don't know what I am doing mainly because I always wear a sweatband. I do that because I sweat a lot when dancing. I love when someone sees me on the floor for the first time and think WHOA!

It's Waltz Time

My favorite dancing experience was when I lived in Georgia. I would babysit my great-granddaughter. We danced to a waltz tune. I would gather the baby in my arms and dance, while holding her. She enjoyed it as well.

TBD

Younger people tell me "I want to be like you when I grow up." I tell them "Just keep dancing."

You Tubing It

I laugh at myself when I mess up! I laugh also when I just can't get a dance.....then I go home and diligently watch YouTube till I get it!

You will Always Be My Star

My late husband was such a fan of Lola Fulana. When I told him I was a bit jealous of his admiration for this beautiful and talented star, he told me "You will Always Be My Star". That always was his favorite message to me - I was HIS Star. My husband passed away at the young age of 34 - over 33 years ago (Dec 5, 1984). Though there are quite a few dances that I enjoy, when I saw the dance - accompanied by that song - I was blown away. It was a message of Love just for me. Everyone who is a member of my Line Dance Family, "Step4Step Soul Line Dancers of New Jersey," KNOWS that is MY dance and they clear the way…(lol). I don't care if I'm dancing by myself, I will always "do" that dance. I truly wish my Beloved Husband and I had discovered this level of line dancing before he passed away. He LOVED to dance and I KNOW he would enjoy it so much as I do.

A FINAL WORD

African dance has left a deep cultural footprint upon people throughout the world. The significance of dance on the continent began a legacy to commemorate a variety of emotions, events, and experiences. The dances learned in Africa continued in a mutated form among Africans throughout the diaspora. Dances such as the Calenda morphed into the cakewalk and the African Gumboot was a predecessor for stepping by fraternities and sororities.

Understanding the connection to our roots and the accomplishments of the continent of Africa is key to embracing heritage, and strength, The Sankofa Bird, looking back to go forward may help one to appreciate the solid foundation upon which many current day practices are built. An image of the Sankofa Bird is attached here. We must embrace our rich history and build upon the wisdom of our ancestors.

The Sankofa Bird

The Sankofa Bird:

*An ancient mythical African bird that flies forward
while looking backward to remind us to remember
our history as we examine the present and look
toward the future.*

The current day health condition of
African Americans is a critical concern.
African Americans are more likely to contract
illnesses such as heart disease, high blood
pressure and obesity. While some of these
ailments may be hereditary or environmental,
many illnesses are due to individual life styles.
Some of these conditions can be prevented or
alleviated through movement. Research has
shown that when comparing dancing to other
forms of exercise such as biking, swimming,
walking or tennis. DANCING is the most
potent exercise with preventative qualities.
The poem that follows this section, written by
one of the Washington Park Senior Line
Dancers, Earnest Barnett Jr., describes how the
motion involved in line dancing and the
synergy among the participants causes positive
energy to flow.

Observations of feeling good, greater
memory and ability to concentrate, greater
strength and endurance were echoed by most
of the dancers. The reports of the dancers
closely mirrored the research regarding the

physical, mental physical and spiritual benefits of dancing. A striking benefit of dancing is the effect of this activity on the brain. Dancing improves memory, as well as concentration ability, and can actually make one smarter! Research confirms that the brain is a muscle, which when used, gets stronger! Dancing requires the use of several receptors in the brain and thus is a preferred activity for making one smarter!

Many may fail to use home remedies of treadmills or videotapes for exercise. It is likely that these solo activities are soon abandoned due to boredom. The collective approach of line dancing, stepping, swing or ballroom dancing perhaps attracts more individuals because of the similarity to the communal approach in Africa. Information on how to get involved in dancing and a few national and local resources are provided in the Addendum.

DANCING is in our DNA. It's time for us to fully embrace the practices of the Motherland that can lend to our improved physical, mental and spiritual health and welfare today.

"And When You Get the Choice to Sit or Dance – I hope You DANCE!"
- Lee Ann Womack

A Tribute To The Washington Park Young at Heart Dancers

These Seniors meet at the Center in Washington Park

They call themselves the Young at Heart

This Senior Group is made up of mostly ladies;

But, men are not excluded.

And, if they come and join,

They will be most graciously included.

The group's motto is: *Keep it Moving*!

Their motive could be: *Keep it Grooving*!

They line dance to the tunes of Rhythm and Blues;

They may be Seniors, but they show youthful moves.

They have added juice to their steps

And spruce to their slide.

And when they perform,

It is with an abundance of pride.

Earnest R. Barnett Jr. , 2015

100

REFERENCES

Adler, R. (2014). *How dance benefits the circulatory system*. In The Healthy Dancer. Available on line: http://thehealthydancer.blogspot.com/2014/02/.

Alpert, P. (2010). *The health benefits of dance: Home health care management & practice.* Vol. 23(2) 155-157. Available on Line: https://doi.org/10.1177/1084822310384689.

Allen V. (2017). Line dancing is better than a walk to fight Alzheimer's: Pensioners who   learn routines are better protected from memory loss and dementia. In Daily Mail: August 25, Available on Line: http://www.dailymail.co.uk/health/article.

American Diabetes Association. (2014). *Treatment & care for African Americans.* Available on Line: http://www.diabetes.org/living-witdiabetes/treatment-and-care/high-risk-populations/treatment-african-americans.html.

American Heart Association. (2015). *African Americans & heart disease, stroke.* Available on Line: http://www.heart.org/HEARTORG/ Conditions/More/MyHeart.

Asante, K.W. (2000). *Zimbabwe dance: Rhythmic forces, ancestral voices, and an aesthetic analysis.* New Jersey: Africa World Press.

Behavioral Risk Factor Surveillance. (2015). Available on Line: https://www.cdc.gov/brfss/annual_da ta/annual.

Brauninger, I. (2016). *It can help substance abuse, PTSD, shyness & more.* Available on Line in Anxiety.org. 2-10-16.

Center for Disease Control (2017). *Health of Black or African American non-Hispanic population.* Available on Line: https://www.cdc.gov/nchs/fastats/bla ck-health.html.

Center for Disease Control (2016). *Health United States 2015 Black or African American population.* Available on Line: https://www.cdc.gov/nchs/hus/black. html.

Center for Disease Control (2015). *African Americans/Blacks. Health Disparities.* Available on Line: https://www.cdc.gov/nchhstp/health disparities.

Crawford, V. (N.D.) *The history of dance.* Available on Line: https://dance.lovetoknow.com/History _of_African_Dance#3fa3yL6mjcYy9Q T3.99.

Green, J. (2005). *Spiritual Resilience.* Indiana: Green Enterprizes Publications.

Halliwell, R. (2016). *Why dancing feels so good.* In The Telegraph. 4-29-16. Available on Line: http://www.telegraph.co.uk/good-news/seven-seas

Hilbring, V. (2017). *More than dance: Here are eight things you need to know about the art of stepping.* Available in Essence on Line: https://www.essence.com/culture/wh at-to-know-history-stepping

Jade, D. (2013). *The African origin of the modern musical instruments: from the fiddle to the gitarro.* Available on line: http://home.earthlink.net/~tshack2/te rmproject/shacklett/goje.htmi

Kattenstroth J-C, Kalisch, T. Holt, S. Tegenthoff, M. & Dinse, H.R. (2013). *Six monthsof dance intervention enhances postural, sensorimotor, and cognitive performance in elderly without affecting cardio-respiratory functions.* In Front. Aging Neuroscience. 5 (5).

Kieft, E. (2014). *Dance as a moving spirituality: A case study of movement medicine.* Volume 1(1). Intellect LTD Article.

Knowles, M. (2017). *Dance your way to beating heart disease, cancer and dementia.* In the Daily Express. (4-10) Available on Line: https://www.pressreader.com/uk/daily-express/20170410/28157806

Lewis, J. (2017). *The history of African dance.* In Flo Dance. Available on Line: https://*www.flodance.com/articles/50665 94-t.*

Lovatt, P. (2016). This is why we dance. In BBC Science Focus. 302 (62-67).

Manning, S. (2014). *Key works, artists, events, venues, texts: Black dance on U.S. stages in the 20th century: Black Arts Initiative.* Available on Line: http://www.bai.northwestern.edu

Matthews, J. (2009). *What are the benefits of dance inspired workouts*. Available in American Council of Exercise.

Nadasen, K. (2008*). Life without line dancing and the other activities would be too dreadful to imagine: An Increase in Social Activity for Older Women*. In Journal of Women & Aging: 20 (3-4): 329-42.

New World Encyclopedia (2016). *African dance*. Available on Line: http://www.newworldencyclopedia.org/p/index.php?title=African_dance&oldid=1001162.

Opoku, A., & Bell, W. (1965). *African dance: A Ghanaian profile*. Legon: University of Ghana.

Paljug, K. (2017). *Health benefits of dancing for seniors; Available in: Your Care Everywhere*. Available on Line: https://www.yourcareeverywhere.com/life-stages/healthy-aging/health-benefits-of-dancing-for-seniors.html.

Powers, R. (2010). *"Use it or lose it: Dancing makes you smarter."* http://socialdance.stanford.edu/syllabi/smarter.html.

Ratey, J. (2008). *Spark: How exercise will improve the performance of your brain.* New York: Little, Brown & Company.

Thompson, R.F. (1974). *African art in motion: Icon & act.* California: University of California Press.

Ward, S, (2008). *Health and the power of dance."* Journal of Physical Education, Recreation and Dance: 79:4.

ADDENDUM

HOW TO GET INVOLVED IN DANCING!

Line, Stepping, and Ballroom Dance Classes are typically tailored to respond to the abilities of the dancers. Classes for beginners, intermediate dancers and advanced participants are often available. Classes may be offered through Parks and Recreation departments, Churches, Civic Centers, YMCA's or through individuals, who teach in their homes or in public arenas. While many groups are inclusive of all ages, others may cater to specific age groups such as youth or seniors. Some dance groups perform at community events. Others might travel, or participate in competitive events. Interested *"dancers to be"* are encouraged to visit several different classes to determine the best fit for them. For those seeking a more individualized approach, many line dances are available via the Internet You-tube videos.

Selected Dance Resources

Universal Line Dancing Group
Provides information regarding line dance activities across the United States
https://www.facebook.com/groups/164844910212525/events/

Steppers USA.Com
Information on Stepping classes across the U.S.
http://www.steppersusa.com/lessons/states/

United Soul Dancers of Florida
2021 N. Lemans Blvd
Tampa, Florida 33607
(803) 537-1113

Diamonds of Déjà vu
Distinguished Men of Déjà vu
4321 Salem Ave
Dayton, Ohio
 (937) 270-3861

Step 4 Step Soul Line Dancers
PO Box 25217
Newark, NJ 07101
S4S@step4steplinedancers.com

California Soul Line Dancers
1906 Pacific Ave
Stockton, California
(209) 598-5097

Selected Indianapolis Line Dance Instructors

Washington Park "Young at Heart" Senior Line Dancers Lilly Woodard, Director 3130 E. 30th Street, Indianapolis, IN 317-501-8621	*Jeanette Barnett* Soul Line Dancing 3908 Meadows Drive Indianapolis, Indiana 317-430-2430	*Ali James* Urban Line Dance Class LimeLight Indy 5150 W 38th St. Indianapolis IN

Dance Information is also available at Indy Parks
Riverside –Will & Patsy Brown
Municipal Gardens – Ray Martin
Windsor Park Village – Jeanette Barnett
https://apm.activecommunities.com/indyparks
317-327-7275

TWELVE TIPS FOR NEW DANCERS

1. Take things one-step at a time.   Give your body time to adjust to the motions, rhythm and music. Build stamina slowly. This is a marathon – not a 50-yard dash!

2. Pay attention to dance instructors. Do not disrupt class with side talking.

3. Stock up on water to replenish your body. Other beverages are less beneficial.

4. Be aware of the personal space needs that you have, as well as those of the other dancers.

5. Tune in to your preferred learning mode. If you are kinesthetic – it may help you to mimic the steps or experience them at the time of demonstration.   If you are auditory, you might benefit from reciting the steps. If you are visual you may need to watch others perform the steps and then jump in or you may need to take notes and review what you've written.

6. Be mindful of your body and what you need. Take a break, as necessary.   You are the best judge of your abilities and limitations.

7. If you need help or to repeat a step, speak up! Chances are others will benefit from the review also.

8. Wear comfortable clothing. Keep it simple.

9. Invest in some good dance shoes. They will get a lot of use. Be good to your feet.

10. Don't be hard on yourself. Remember the only mistake is not to try.

11. Get to know the other dancers. This is a community with mutual interests.

12. Be able to laugh at yourself. Try not to take things so seriously. Have fun!

"If you can talk, you can sing. And if you can walk, you can DANCE."
– African Proverb

AFRICAN COUNTRIES: TYPES OF DANCES AND PURPOSE

Country/Tribe	Dance	Purpose
1. Cameroon	Ambas-i-bay	Celebration
2. Cameroon	Bikutsi	Celebration
3. Cameroon	Makossa	Celebration
4. Congo (DRC)	Kwassa kwassa	Celebration
5. Cote d'Ivoire	Coupe'-Decale'	Celebration
6. Cote d'Ivoire	Mapouka	Ceremonial
7. Ghana/Ashanti	Adowa	Funeral Dance
8. Ghana/Ewe	Agbaja	Ritual
9. Ghana /Ashanti	Kete	Funeral, War
10. Guinea	Lamban	Celebration
11. Guinea	Kakilabe	Fertility
12. Mali	Lamban	Celebration
13. Mali/Baga people	Kakilambe	Fertility

Country/Tribe	Dance	Purpose
14. Senegal	Gombey	Harvest
15. Senegal	Lamban	Celebration
16. Uganda/Acholi	Bwola	Celebration
17. Uganda/Acholi	Larakaraka	Courtship
18. Uganda /Acholi	Ding DIng	Community
19. Uganda/Alur	Agwara	Courtship
20. Uganda/Bagisu	Mwaga	Courtship
21. Uganda/Bakiga	Ekizino	Courtship
22. Uganda/ Bayankole	Ekitaguriro	Harvest
23. Uganda/Banyoro	Entogoro	Glaze
24. Uganda/Buganda	Bakisimba	Celebration
25. Uganda/Buganda	Amaggunju	Royalty
26. Uganda/Iteso	Akogo	Courtship
27. Uganda/ Lugbara	Entog	Gaze

DANCE SURVEY UTILIZED FOR THIS PUBLICATION

A copy of the letter inviting dancers to participate is included here. Letters and surveys were distributed in person and at a variety of dance locations. Invitation letters and surveys and were also provided on line. A copy of the letter of invite and the survey are included for your information.

GRE EN TERPRIZES

Dr. Jacqualyn Green

Request for Dancers !!!

Dear Dancer,

I am an avid line dancer and a researcher. I have been line dancing for several years and thoroughly enjoy the music, motion and the fellowship that accompanies this activity. I have been intrigued regarding the magnitude of this craze around the United States, particularly among older African Americans. I am interested in identifying what attracts people to this activity, the type of dance and the degree to which they are involved in dance, as well as any physical, mental, or spiritual benefits experienced due to dancing!

If dancing plays a significant role in your life and you would like to share your experience, please complete the survey that follows. Your sentiments may inspire others to embrace this positive lifestyle!

While we are unable to pay you for your contribution, if your information is included in the upcoming publication, you will be given acknowledgement in the book regarding the benefits of dance, unless you would prefer to remain anonymous. You will also receive several copies of the final publication.

You may return your survey in person, by e-mail, fax, or snail mail. *All* contact information is listed below. The survey is also available on my website: https://www.green-enterprizes.com. I can also e-mail you the link if you provide your e-mail address. I hope that you will participate in this endeavor which may encourage African Americans to adopt more positive health practices in their lifestyle.

Thank you for your consideration,

Dr. Jacqualyn Green
Line dancer, who is learning ballroom and enjoying stepping!

Why We Dance Survey

1. Name

```
┌─────────────────────────────────────────┐
│                                         │
│                                         │
└─────────────────────────────────────────┘
```

2. Gender
  a. [ ] Male
  b. [ ] Female

3. Where do you live?

_____

city   state

4. Which age category fits you?
a. [ ] under 25
b. [ ] 25-35
c. [ ] 36-46
d. [ ] 47-57
e. [ ] 58-68
f. [ ] 69-79
g. [ ] 80+

5. Please Provide your Employment Status

Working / If working, what type of work do you do?

_____

Retired / If retired, what type of work did you do?

_____

Semi-Retired / Number of hours worked per week

Other: Please specify

---

6. How long have you been dancing?
a. [ ] 5 years or less
b. [ ] 6-10 years
c. [ ] 11-15 years
d. [ ] 16-20 years
e. [ ] 21-25 years
f. [ ] 26-30 years0
g. [ ] 31 years or more
h. [ ] Other/ Please specify.

---

7. What type of dancing do you do?
a. [ ] Line Dancing
b. [ ] Stepping
c. [ ] Ball Room
d. [ ] Swing Dancing
e. [ ] Other/ Please specify.

---

8. How often do you dance?
a. [ ] Daily
b. [ ] Three-Four times a week
c. [ ] Twice a Week
d. [ ] Once a Week
e. [ ] Twice a Month
f. [ ] Once a Month
g. [ ] Other/ Please Specify

---

9. What is your Favorite Dance?

_____

Why?

_____
_____
_____

10. How did you first get interested in dancing?

_____
_____
_____

11. What (if any) physical benefits have you
noticed from dancing? Please describe.

_____
_____
_____

12. What (if any) mental benefits have you
noticed from dancing? Please describe.

_____
_____
_____

13. What (if any) spiritual benefits have you
noticed from dancing? Please describe.

_____
_____
_____

14. Are there any downsides to dancing? If so, please describe

_____
_____
_____

15. If you would like to share a favorite or funny dancing experience, please do so here.

_____
_____
_____
_____
_____
_____
_____

Thank you for your participation in this survey. Your responses will inform us regarding how dance is affecting African Americans. You will be notified regarding the use of your survey and the completion of this project.

Dr. Jacqualyn F. Green

For the Reader: Please use the following pages to identify your dance strengths, challenges and potential dance goals. This information may be useful to anyone who is considering a dance class, dance activities or other forms of exercise. Self-examination and goal setting may help potential dancers to move from "thinking about dancing" to Getting On the DANCE FLOOR!

MY DANCE STRENGTHS

Which dance moves are you good at? Does dancing come easily for you? Do you practice until you "have it?" Do you have a history of dancing? Are there incentives to keep you dancing i.e. friends who dance in the group, convenient location, hours that fit into your life style? Please describe.

_____
_____
_____
_____
_____
_____
_____
_____
_____
_____
_____

MY DANCE CHALLENGES

Think about what could get in your way. Are you coordinated? Do you begin activities and give up soon afterwards? Do you lose interest quickly? Do you have two left feet? Do you have other responsibilities? Are you able to carve out time – just for you?

_____
_____
_____
_____
_____
_____
_____
_____
_____
_____
_____
_____

DANCES I'D LIKE TO LEARN

_____
_____
_____
_____
_____
_____
_____
_____
_____
_____
_____

ABOUT THE AUTHOR

Dr. Jacqualyn F. Green is the founder of Green Enterprizes, a counseling, consulting and training firm established in Indianapolis, in1983. She has worked nationally and internationally, providing seminars on cultural diversity, leadership skills, generational challenges, and spiritual understanding. Dr. Green has a Bachelor Degree in Psychology from Fisk University in Nashville, Tennessee and Masters and Doctorate degrees in Social Work from Indiana University.

Her first book, *Spiritual Resilience* was based upon her own spiritual journey, questions posed by clients and friends, and colleagues, through the years, and learnings from her trips throughout the United States, as well as to many countries in Africa, the Caribbean, Europe, and Canada.

Her second book, *Racial Resilience* is the outgrowth of her dissertation, which captured African American student experiences and recommendations regarding success in HBCU's (Historically Black Colleges & Universities) and PWI's (Predominantly White Institutions). In this publication, Dr. Green introduced a concept that is often overlooked in the college setting, the ability of the student and the institution to respond to individual or organizational racial challenges.

Her third publication, *Grandmama Mama Drama* details the custody battle that many parents and grandparents encounter when attempting to provide a safe and nurturing environment for children. Grandparent roles, strengths, challenges, resources, and personal stories from grandparents are captured in this book.

Dr. Green is a regular contributor to the *Black Child Journal* and an annual presenter at the International Black Women's Congress (IBWC), The Black Writers Events (BWE), and the Consortium of Doctors (COD). Each year, Dr. Green convenes the Authors and Friends Panel at Fisk University.

Dr. Green is married, with two sons and three grandchildren. She attributes her success to God, her ancestors, particularly her parents, who have ascended, and to her family who has assisted in this writing effort, as well as in every endeavor she has undertaken.

It is Dr. Green's hope that by reading *Dance! It's in your DNA*, readers will learn more about their culture, the benefits of dancing, the positive experiences of dancers and will be moved to DANCE!

"You know you're a dancer when "and" is a number."

ORDER INFORMATION

There are two ways to order information. Please visit the Green Enterprizes website to make purchases on line, or use the Order Form on the next page to purchase these publications by mail.

TO ORDER COPIES of the following publications on line, please visit the Green Enterprizes Website: https: www.green-enterprizes.com

_____Dance! It's in Your DNA! ($16.00)

_____Grandmama Mama Drama $16.00)

_____Spiritual Resilience ($14.95)

_____Spiritual Resilience: The Workbook ($10.00)

_____Racial Resilience ($14.95)

_____Racial Resilience: The Workbook ($10.00)

_____Healing Black Women from Violence ($20.00)

_____2014-2016 Issues of Black Child Journals ($20 per issue) _Please Specify Issue._

Payments are accepted from American Express, Discover, Master Card or Visa. _Please Call:_ (317) 257-6773 for additional information.

Complete and Mail this ORDER FORM to purchase by mail.

Name:

_____

Address:

_____

City _____

State _____ Zip _____

Please Specify Number of copies:

_____Dance! It's in Your DNA! ($16.00)

_____Grandmama Mama Drama $16.00)

_____Spiritual Resilience ($14.95)

_____Spiritual Resilience: The Workbook ($10.00)

_____Racial Resilience ($14.95)

_____Racial Resilience: The Workbook ($10.00)

_____Healing Black Women from Violence ($20.00)

_____2014-2016 Issues of Black Child Journals ($20 per issue)

_____

Please specify Issue

To cover postage, please add $2.00 for the first book and $1.00 for each additional book

Make check payable to **Dr. Jacqualyn F. Green**

Payments are also accepted from: American Express, Discover, Master Card or Visa.

If using a charge card please include:
Your name as it appears on card:

_____

Expiration Date_____(month, year)
Security Code_____ (3 or 4 digit number)

Your
Signature_____

Your phone number or e-mail address

_____

TOTAL AMOUNT ENCLOSED: $ _____

Mail Check, Order Information & Order Form to:
Green Enterprizes Publications
4755 Kingsway Drive Suite 308
Indianapolis, Indiana 46205

Please call: (317) 257-6773 for additional information.

DANCE! It's In Your DNA

DANCE! It's In Your DNA